CONTENTS

THE UK UNLOCKED:

A SHORT GUIDE TO TRAVELLING AND SELLING IN THE UK

J K Lewis

Introduction

The United Kingdom (UK) is a land steeped in history and tradition, where the old meets the new in an exciting fusion of culture, commerce, and opportunity. From the bustling streets of London, the financial heart of Europe, to the creative, entrepreneurial hubs of Manchester and Edinburgh, the UK offers a rich, diverse marketplace for both established businesses and budding entrepreneurs.

Whether you are travelling the country selling artisanal products at local markets or launching a new business in the competitive online space, the UK is brimming with potential. But success here requires more than just a quality product or service. To thrive in the UK, you must understand its unique consumer culture, navigate its highly organised transport systems, and tailor your business to the specific needs of British buyers.

This guide is designed to help you do just that. Whether you are exploring the urban opportunities in cities like London, Birmingham, or Glasgow, or discovering the growing interest in sustainable and local products in rural areas, this book provides all the information you need to make your venture a success.

Why the UK?

The UK is one of the world's leading economies and a key player in global commerce, making it an attractive destination for entrepreneurs. British consumers are discerning and value quality, innovation, and sustainability. With a population of over 67 million and a strong appetite for new products and services, the UK is an ideal market for businesses of all sizes.

The country's strategic position in Europe, combined with its extensive transport infrastructure, makes it easy to move between cities and regions, enabling businesses to reach a broad and diverse customer base. Additionally, the UK's online retail sector is one of the largest in the world, offering significant opportunities for businesses looking to expand digitally.

What You'll Learn

In this guide, we'll take you through every step of travelling and selling in the UK, from understanding the cultural and regional differences that shape consumer behaviour, to mastering the logistics of moving your goods across the country. We'll explore both traditional markets and fairs, as well as the ever-growing e-commerce landscape, providing practical advice on how to set up your business, manage taxes, and comply with UK regulations.

You'll learn how to:

- **Navigate the UK's geography and consumer culture**, identifying the best places to sell your products and understanding the tastes and preferences of British buyers.
- **Travel efficiently across the country**, using the UK's extensive public transport and road networks, and choosing the best accommodation options for your business trips.
- **Set up your business in the UK**, with guidance on choosing the right business structure, registering for VAT, and staying compliant with local regulations.
- **Sell at markets and fairs**, from securing a spot at one of London's famous street markets to participating

in regional fairs across Scotland, Wales, and Northern Ireland.

- **Build a successful e-commerce presence**, by optimising your online store for British consumers and learning the best digital marketing strategies to reach your target audience.

- **Develop strong business relationships** by understanding British business etiquette, from formal meetings to informal networking events, and learning how to build long-term connections with UK clients and partners.

A Diverse and Evolving Market

The UK is a country of contrasts. It is home to London, one of the most cosmopolitan cities in the world, and yet rural traditions are deeply rooted in its smaller towns and villages. Each region of the UK has its own distinct identity and cultural nuances, which can influence the products and services that resonate with local consumers. This guide will help you identify these regional differences and adjust your approach to maximise your impact in every part of the country.

In recent years, British consumers have increasingly favoured sustainable, locally sourced products. Artisanal goods, eco-friendly fashion, and organic food and drink are all growing markets. This shift provides significant opportunities for businesses that can meet these demands with quality, ethical products.

Embrace the Opportunity

Travelling and selling in the UK is an exciting journey, filled with opportunities to grow your business and connect with a diverse, sophisticated consumer base. The UK rewards those who adapt to its unique market dynamics, understand its culture, and provide the quality and innovation that British buyers expect.

Whether you're starting a small enterprise or expanding an established business, *the UK Unlocked: A Short Guide to Travelling and Selling in the United Kingdom* will equip you with the knowledge and tools you need to navigate this dynamic market with confidence.

Now, let's dive into the UK's regions and consumer landscape to begin your journey towards business success in the United Kingdom!

CHAPTER 1: THE GEOGRAPHY AND CULTURE OF THE UNITED KINGDOM

The United Kingdom (UK) is a country of rich cultural diversity and varying regional characteristics. Made up of four nations—England, Scotland, Wales, and Northern Ireland—the UK offers a range of consumer behaviours, preferences, and business opportunities depending on where you choose to sell. Understanding the geography and culture of the UK is essential to effectively targeting your products and tailoring your approach to meet the specific needs of British consumers.

In this chapter, we will explore the different regions of the UK, their economic and cultural distinctions, and how these differences can influence your business strategy.

1.1 Overview of the UK's Regions

The UK is divided into distinct regions, each with its own cultural identity, economic strengths, and consumer preferences. Your business strategy may need to adapt depending on the region in which you are selling, as buying habits, preferences, and markets can vary widely.

England

England is the largest of the four nations, both in terms of population and economic power. Its regions vary significantly, from the bustling metropolis of London to the industrial heartlands of the North. England's diverse economy offers opportunities across a broad range of sectors, but success often depends on understanding the regional nuances that influence consumer behaviour.

- **London**: The UK's capital is a global financial hub and one of the most cosmopolitan cities in the world. Londoners have a taste for high-end products, luxury goods, and innovative services. If you're selling fashion, tech, or premium artisanal goods, London is a prime market, but it is also one of the most competitive.

- **The South East**: This region is known for its affluence and proximity to London. It includes cities like **Oxford**, **Brighton**, and **Reading**. Consumers here are often well-travelled and tend to favour sustainable and luxury products. High-tech, finance, and education are key sectors.

- **The North West**: Cities like **Manchester** and **Liverpool** are major economic centres in the North West. Manchester is a growing hub for media and technology, while Liverpool's maritime history still influences its economy. Both cities have a rich cultural scene, and consumers in this region are price-conscious but open to high-quality, innovative products.

- **The Midlands**: The Midlands, including cities like **Birmingham**, **Coventry**, and **Leicester**, has a strong industrial heritage. Known as the UK's manufacturing heartland, it is home to a significant portion of the country's automotive, aerospace, and engineering industries. Birmingham, the largest city in the Midlands, has a diverse consumer base, and the market for affordable, practical goods thrives here.

Scotland

Scotland, with its dramatic landscapes and rich cultural history, has a distinct national identity within the UK. The major economic centres of **Edinburgh** and **Glasgow** offer vibrant marketplaces for a range of industries, including finance, technology, and food and drink. Scotland's rural areas are also well-known for their high-quality agricultural products and artisanal crafts.

- **Edinburgh**: As the capital of Scotland, Edinburgh is a major financial hub and cultural centre. It is home to the **Edinburgh Festival**, one of the world's largest arts festivals, which draws international tourists and local consumers alike. The city's residents are affluent and value both traditional craftsmanship and cutting-edge innovation.

- **Glasgow**: Scotland's largest city, Glasgow, has a strong industrial past but is now a creative and tech-driven hub. It is known for its vibrant music and arts scene, and businesses that sell affordable, trendy, and innovative products often thrive here.

- **The Highlands and Islands**: Scotland's rural areas are famous for their natural beauty, tourism, and traditional industries, such as whisky production, fishing, and agriculture. Markets here often focus on local products, including artisanal crafts, food, and drink.

Wales

Wales is known for its scenic landscapes, with a strong cultural identity rooted in the Welsh language, music, and tradition. The country has a growing creative and media sector, as well as a robust tourism industry. Wales presents a unique opportunity for businesses selling local, sustainable, and handcrafted goods.

- **Cardiff**: As the capital of Wales, Cardiff is the main economic centre and home to a burgeoning creative sector. The city is also known for its sporting events, with **Principality Stadium** hosting rugby matches that draw huge crowds. Cardiff's consumer market values affordable, well-designed goods, with a growing interest in sustainability and locally made products.

- **Swansea and Rural Wales**: Swansea, another major city,

has a growing tech and innovation sector. Meanwhile, rural Wales is an excellent market for businesses selling handcrafted or artisanal products, particularly those with a focus on sustainability or local sourcing.

Northern Ireland

Northern Ireland's economy is smaller than the other nations within the UK but offers niche opportunities, particularly in tourism, technology, and food and drink. **Belfast**, the capital, is a hub for innovation, while smaller towns and rural areas provide opportunities for artisanal and locally sourced products.

- **Belfast**: Northern Ireland's largest city is known for its growing tech and innovation sectors. Belfast has a dynamic startup scene, particularly in fintech and cybersecurity. Consumer preferences here favour innovation and practicality, with a growing focus on locally sourced and sustainable products.

- **Rural Northern Ireland**: The rural areas of Northern Ireland are known for high-quality agricultural products, including dairy and beef. Markets in these regions often focus on artisanal crafts and locally made goods, with an emphasis on heritage and tradition.

1.2 Urban vs. Rural Markets

The contrast between urban and rural markets in the UK is significant, and understanding the different consumer behaviours in these areas can help you tailor your approach. Urban areas tend to have more affluent, tech-savvy consumers, while rural markets are often more focused on local, artisanal products.

Urban Markets

The UK's major cities, including London, Birmingham, Manchester, and Glasgow, are hubs of commerce and culture. These cities attract a mix of professionals, students, and tourists, creating diverse and competitive markets. Urban consumers tend to be early adopters of new technology and trends, with a growing interest in sustainability, ethical sourcing, and innovative design.

- **What Sells**: Fashion, tech gadgets, sustainable goods, high-end food and drink, and premium services are all popular in urban markets.

Rural Markets

Rural areas in the UK, such as the Scottish Highlands, the Cotswolds, and the Welsh valleys, are characterised by tight-knit communities and a focus on locally made goods. These areas are often hubs for tourism, with visitors seeking out artisanal products and unique experiences.

- **What Sells**: Locally sourced food, artisanal crafts, handmade jewellery, and traditional textiles are particularly popular in rural markets. Products with a strong connection to the local culture or environment tend to do well.

1.3 Understanding UK Consumer Culture

British consumers are sophisticated and price-conscious but also value quality and sustainability. Understanding their priorities and cultural preferences can help you position your products effectively.

Quality and Craftsmanship

British buyers appreciate well-made, durable goods. Whether you're selling fashion, home goods, or food, emphasising the quality of your materials and the craftsmanship behind your products can set you apart from competitors.

Sustainability and Ethics

Sustainability is a growing concern for UK consumers, particularly among younger buyers. Products that are eco-friendly, ethically sourced, or made with minimal environmental impact are highly valued. Offering transparency about your sourcing and production methods will resonate with British consumers.

Value for Money

Price-consciousness is a key factor for many UK consumers. While they are willing to pay more for quality, they also expect value for their money. Offering competitive prices or showcasing the long-term value of your products can help attract more cost-conscious buyers.

The Importance of Tradition

British consumers often favour products with a sense of tradition or heritage, especially in markets like food, drink, and crafts. Highlighting the history or cultural significance of your products can create a deeper connection with buyers, particularly in rural areas or when selling at traditional markets.

Chapter 1 - Summary

Understanding the diverse geography and culture of the United Kingdom is essential for tailoring your business strategy to each region. From the cosmopolitan streets of London to the traditional rural markets of Wales and Scotland, the UK offers a wide range of consumer preferences and opportunities. By adapting your approach to fit the specific characteristics of each region, you'll be better positioned to succeed in this dynamic and varied marketplace

CHAPTER 2: THE LOGISTICS OF TRAVELLING IN THE UK

The United Kingdom has an extensive and well-maintained transport network that makes travelling between cities and regions efficient and relatively easy. Whether you're planning to attend markets in different cities, meet clients across the country, or explore new regions to sell your products, the UK offers a variety of transport options. In this chapter, we'll explore the best ways to travel across the UK, including trains, car rentals, public transport, and accommodation options for business travellers.

2.1 Transportation Options

When it comes to travelling in the UK, there are several reliable options available, depending on your destination, budget, and the amount of goods you need to transport. Each option has its benefits, and choosing the right one for your business needs can save you time and money.

Train Travel: Fast and Convenient

The UK has an extensive and efficient rail network, which connects major cities and towns, making it an excellent option for business travellers who need to move quickly between locations. **National Rail** services cover the entire country, with some high-speed options available for key routes, such as **London to Manchester** or **Edinburgh to Glasgow**.

- **High-Speed Rail**: Services such as **Virgin Trains**, **Avanti West Coast**, and **LNER** offer fast travel between major cities. For example, the journey from London to Manchester takes around 2 hours and from London to Edinburgh around 4.5 hours. These services are ideal if you're travelling between large cities and want to avoid the hassle of driving.

- **Regional Trains**: If you're travelling to smaller towns or rural areas, regional train services such as **ScotRail** in Scotland, **Great Western Railway** in the South West, or **Transport for Wales** in Wales are reliable options. These trains offer more localised routes, making them ideal for reaching smaller markets or remote areas.

- **Rail Passes**: Consider investing in a **Railcard** or regional rail passes if you plan to travel frequently by train. These passes can save you money by offering unlimited travel over a certain period, making them ideal for entrepreneurs travelling extensively across the UK.

Car Rentals: Flexibility for Reaching Remote Markets

Renting a car gives you the flexibility to travel at your own pace and reach areas where public transport may not be as convenient. This is particularly useful if you're travelling with a large amount of inventory or planning to attend markets in rural locations.

- **Renting a Car**: There are many car rental companies available in the UK, including **Hertz**, **Enterprise**, and **Europcar**, with locations in major cities and airports. Renting a car or van is a practical option if you're transporting large quantities of goods between locations or attending markets in different regions.

- **Driving in the UK**: The UK's roads are generally well-maintained, and the motorway system (indicated by **M** roads) connects major cities and regions. Keep in mind that the UK drives on the left-hand side of the road, which may take some getting used to if you're accustomed to driving on the right. Additionally, many motorways are toll-free, but some bridges and tunnels may require a toll payment.

- **Parking and Low Emission Zones**: In cities, parking can be expensive and limited, especially in London, which also has a **Congestion Charge** zone. Be aware of **Low Emission Zones (LEZ)** in cities like London, Birmingham, and Glasgow, which charge older, more polluting vehicles for entry. If you're renting a vehicle, ensure that it meets the emissions standards for the areas you'll be visiting.

Public Transport in Cities

If you're primarily travelling within a city, public transport offers a convenient and cost-effective way to move around. Major cities like London, Manchester, and Glasgow have comprehensive public transport systems that include buses, trams, and underground trains.

- **London Underground (Tube)**: London's Tube system is one of the most efficient ways to travel across the city. With 11 lines covering central London and the suburbs, it connects key business districts and shopping areas. Consider getting an **Oyster card** or using contactless payment for quick access to the Tube, buses, and trams.

- **Trams and Buses**: Other cities like **Manchester**, **Edinburgh**, and **Nottingham** have excellent tram systems, which are an affordable way to reach different parts of the city. Buses are also a reliable option for urban travel, and most cities have dedicated bus lanes to ensure efficiency.

- **Taxis and Ride-Hailing**: **Black cabs** in London and other cities are a convenient option for quick travel, though they can be expensive. Ride-hailing apps like **Uber**, **Bolt**, and **Ola** operate in most UK cities, offering a more affordable alternative to traditional taxis.

2.2 Accommodations for Travelling Entrepreneurs

When travelling for business, choosing the right accommodation can make your trip more productive and comfortable. The UK offers a variety of lodging options, ranging from budget-friendly hotels to short-term rentals that provide the space to store inventory and work efficiently.

Short-Term Rentals (Airbnb, Vrbo)

For extended stays or if you need more space to store products, short-term rentals through platforms like **Airbnb** or **Vrbo** can be a great option. Renting an apartment or house gives you access to amenities like kitchens and laundry facilities, allowing you to save on meals and manage your day-to-day needs more comfortably. These properties are available across the UK, from major cities to rural towns.

Business Hotels

Business hotels are ideal for short stays and provide the amenities you need to stay productive. Popular hotel chains like **Premier Inn**, **Travelodge**, and **Hilton** have locations throughout the UK and offer services such as free Wi-Fi, business centres, and meeting rooms.

- **Premier Inn and Travelodge**: Both of these budget-friendly hotel chains offer clean, comfortable rooms at reasonable prices. They are a popular choice for business travellers looking for centrally located accommodation with essential amenities.

- **Hilton, Marriott, and Novotel**: For more upscale options, hotels like **Hilton** and **Marriott** provide higher-end amenities, including executive lounges, fitness centres, and larger meeting spaces. These hotels are often located in key business districts, making them convenient for meetings or events.

Bed & Breakfasts (B&Bs)

If you're travelling to rural areas or smaller towns, traditional

Bed & Breakfasts (B&Bs) are a charming and cost-effective option. B&Bs typically offer a more personal experience and often include breakfast, which can be a great way to start your day before heading to a market or meeting. They are especially common in regions like **Cornwall**, **Yorkshire**, and **Scotland**.

2.3 Organising the Transport of Goods

Managing the transport of your products efficiently is crucial when travelling and selling across the UK. Whether you're delivering goods to customers, shipping inventory to markets, or fulfilling online orders, having a reliable logistics plan will ensure your business runs smoothly.

Shipping Goods via Couriers

If you're selling online or need to ship products between locations, using couriers is often the most reliable option. The UK has a variety of courier services that offer both domestic and international shipping.

- **Royal Mail**: The UK's national postal service, **Royal Mail**, offers a range of options for businesses, including **1st Class** and **Tracked & Signed** delivery services. Royal Mail is a reliable and cost-effective option for smaller parcels and e-commerce businesses.

- **Private Couriers**: For larger shipments or time-sensitive deliveries, private couriers like **DHL**, **UPS**, and **DPD** provide fast and reliable services. They offer a range of shipping solutions, including same-day delivery, which is useful for high-value or urgent goods.

Transporting Goods Yourself

If you're travelling with a significant amount of inventory to sell at markets or events, renting a van or larger vehicle may be necessary. Many car rental companies in the UK offer cargo vans or trucks designed for business use. Ensure you plan your routes carefully, taking into account any congestion charges or parking restrictions, especially in larger cities.

Click-and-Collect Services

For businesses with an online presence, offering **click-and-collect** services can be a great way to bridge the gap between e-commerce and in-person selling. Many British consumers prefer to order online and collect their items from a nearby location, reducing delivery costs and wait times. Partnering with local shops or using service points like those provided by **CollectPlus** or **InPost** can help facilitate this option.

Chapter 2 - Summary

Travelling in the UK as a business owner is made easy by the country's comprehensive transport network. Whether you're moving between markets, attending meetings, or delivering products to customers, the UK offers a variety of transportation options that suit different needs. By planning your trips efficiently and selecting the right accommodation, you can make your business journey across the UK smooth and productive

CHAPTER 3: SETTING UP YOUR BUSINESS IN THE UK

Setting up a business in the United Kingdom is a relatively straightforward process, thanks to the country's supportive business environment and clear regulations. The UK is one of the most entrepreneurial-friendly markets in Europe, offering various business structures to suit different types of ventures. In this chapter, we will walk you through the steps of choosing the right business structure, registering your company, understanding the tax system, and complying with UK regulations.

3.1 Choosing Your Business Structure

The UK offers several business structures, each with its own advantages and legal requirements. Choosing the right structure is essential for managing your taxes, liabilities, and administrative responsibilities effectively.

Sole Trader

A **sole trader** is the simplest and most common business structure in the UK, particularly for small businesses, freelancers, and self-employed individuals. As a sole trader, you run the business as an individual and are personally responsible for its debts. While this structure offers simplicity, it does not provide any separation between your personal and business finances.

- **Advantages**: Easy to set up, minimal paperwork, and full control over business decisions.
- **Disadvantages**: Personal liability for business debts and taxes.

- **How to Register**: To become a sole trader, you must register with **HM Revenue & Customs (HMRC)** for self-assessment and file an annual tax return. You'll also need to register for **Value-Added Tax (VAT)** if your turnover exceeds the VAT threshold, currently £85,000 per year (as of 2024).

Limited Company (Ltd)

A **Limited Company (Ltd)** is a separate legal entity from its owners, offering limited liability. This means that the business itself is responsible for its debts, not the shareholders. An Ltd is the most popular structure for businesses looking to scale, raise investment, or protect personal assets.

- **Advantages**: Limited liability, easier to raise capital, and more credibility with customers and suppliers.

- **Disadvantages**: More paperwork, higher administrative costs, and stricter regulations.

- **How to Register**: To register a limited company, you must submit an application to **Companies House**, providing details such as your company's name, address, and the names of directors and shareholders. You'll also need to file annual accounts and a confirmation statement each year. Additionally, you'll need to register for **Corporation Tax** with HMRC.

Partnerships

A **Partnership** is an arrangement where two or more individuals run a business together. There are two main types of partnerships: a **general partnership** and a **limited liability partnership (LLP)**. In a general partnership, all partners share equal responsibility for the business's liabilities, while in an LLP, liability is limited to the amount of money each partner has invested in the business.

- **Advantages**: Shared responsibility, combined skills and resources.

- **Disadvantages**: Personal liability (for general partnerships) and potential for disputes between partners.

- **How to Register**: Partnerships must be registered with HMRC, and each partner will need to submit a self-assessment tax return. If you choose an LLP, it must also be registered with Companies House, and annual accounts must be filed.

Social Enterprises

For businesses that aim to make a positive social or environmental impact, a **social enterprise** may be the right choice. In the UK, a social enterprise can take the form of a **Community Interest Company (CIC)** or a **charity**. These structures allow businesses to pursue social goals while benefiting from certain tax advantages and grants.

- **Advantages**: Access to grants and funding opportunities, credibility with socially conscious consumers.

- **Disadvantages**: Regulated structure with restrictions on profit distribution.

- **How to Register**: A CIC must be registered with Companies House and file annual reports on how it benefits the community. Charities must also register with the **Charity Commission** and adhere to strict regulations regarding the use of funds.

3.2 Managing Taxes and VAT (Value-Added Tax)

Understanding the UK's tax system is crucial to staying compliant and ensuring that your business operates smoothly. The primary taxes for businesses in the UK are **Income Tax** (for sole traders), **Corporation Tax** (for limited companies), and **VAT**.

Income Tax (for Sole Traders)

If you operate as a sole trader, you will pay **Income Tax** on your business profits. Income Tax rates in the UK are progressive, meaning that you pay a higher percentage of tax as your income increases.

- **Tax Bands (as of 2024)**:
  - **Basic rate**: 20% on income between £12,571 and £50,270
  - **Higher rate**: 40% on income between £50,271 and £125,140
  - **Additional rate**: 45% on income above £125,140

As a sole trader, you will also be responsible for paying **National Insurance Contributions (NICs)** based on your profits.

Corporation Tax (for Limited Companies)

If you run a limited company, you will pay **Corporation Tax** on your company's profits. The current rate of Corporation Tax is 25% (as of 2024). Unlike sole traders, limited companies do not pay Income Tax, but directors and shareholders may need to pay **Income Tax** on dividends they receive from the company.

- **How to Pay Corporation Tax**: You must register your company for Corporation Tax with HMRC and file a **Company Tax Return (CT600)** each year. Corporation Tax must be paid within 9 months and 1 day after the end of your company's financial year.

VAT (Value-Added Tax)

VAT is a tax on goods and services that businesses charge to customers. If your turnover exceeds £85,000 per year (the VAT threshold as of 2024), you must register for VAT with HMRC. Even if your turnover is below this threshold, you can voluntarily register for VAT if it benefits your business.

- **VAT Rates**:
  - **Standard rate**: 20%
  - **Reduced rate**: 5% (for certain goods like energy-saving products)
  - **Zero rate**: 0% (for goods like children's clothing and most food)
- **VAT Returns**: Once registered, you must file VAT returns every quarter and pay any VAT you owe to HMRC. Many

businesses use accounting software to automate this process and ensure compliance.

3.3 Understanding UK Consumer Protection Laws

Consumer protection laws in the UK are stringent, ensuring that buyers receive fair treatment and high-quality products. These laws are particularly important if you sell directly to consumers (B2C) or operate an e-commerce business.

Right to Return

Under the **Consumer Contracts Regulations**, UK customers have the right to return most goods purchased online or over the phone within 14 days of receiving them, even if they simply change their mind. You are required to issue a full refund, including standard delivery costs.

Product Safety

All goods sold in the UK must meet strict safety standards. If you sell products such as electronics, toys, or food, they must comply with specific regulations, such as **CE** or **UKCA** marking (for safety compliance), and the **Food Standards Agency (FSA)** rules for food items.

- **Labelling**: Products must be clearly labelled, with all relevant information, including ingredients (for food), allergens, and instructions for use.

Warranties and Guarantees

Under the **Consumer Rights Act 2015**, customers are entitled to goods that are fit for purpose, of satisfactory quality, and as described. If a product is faulty, customers have the right to a repair, replacement, or refund within the first 30 days of purchase.

Data Protection (GDPR)

If your business collects personal data from customers, you must comply with the **General Data Protection Regulation (GDPR)**, which governs how personal data is collected, stored, and used. This is particularly important for e-commerce businesses and those that use customer databases for marketing.

- **Privacy Policy**: Make sure your business has a clear privacy policy that informs customers how their data will be used. Customers must also have the right to request that their data be deleted.

Chapter 3 - Summary

Setting up a business in the UK is a streamlined process, with a variety of business structures to suit different needs and an efficient tax system to ensure compliance. Whether you're a sole trader looking for a simple setup or planning to scale as a limited company, understanding the tax obligations and consumer protection laws is crucial to running a successful business in the UK. With the right structure and attention to detail, you can build a solid foundation for your business and thrive in the British market.

CHAPTER 4: WHAT TO SELL IN THE UK: MARKET INSIGHTS

The United Kingdom's consumer market is diverse, sophisticated, and driven by trends ranging from sustainability to technology. To succeed in the UK, it's essential to understand what products resonate with British buyers, which industries are thriving, and how regional and seasonal trends can affect demand. Whether you're selling fashion, artisanal crafts, or cutting-edge tech products, understanding these insights will help you tailor your offerings to British tastes.

In this chapter, we'll explore the most popular product categories, identify key trends shaping the UK market, and highlight regional and seasonal variations that can influence your sales strategy.

4.1 Best-Selling Product Categories

British consumers are known for their appreciation of quality, craftsmanship, and innovation. The following categories represent some of the best-performing sectors in the UK, providing excellent opportunities for entrepreneurs and small businesses alike.

Fashion and Apparel

The UK is a global fashion hub, with London at the heart of international fashion. British consumers, particularly in urban areas, are known for their sense of style and willingness to embrace both high street and designer brands. The fashion market in the UK caters to a broad range of tastes, from luxury to affordable everyday wear.

- **What Sells**: Clothing, shoes, accessories, and jewellery perform well in the UK, particularly if they are on-trend or offer unique designs. Sustainable fashion is gaining momentum, with eco-conscious consumers looking for ethically produced, durable, and environmentally friendly clothing.

- **Where to Sell**: Fashion products are popular both online and in physical stores, with London, Manchester, and Birmingham being key fashion hubs. Markets such as **Camden Market** in London and online platforms like **ASOS Marketplace** are excellent venues for selling fashion, particularly for independent brands.

Artisanal Goods and Crafts

The UK has a growing market for artisanal products, particularly those that emphasise craftsmanship, local sourcing, and sustainability. From handmade jewellery and pottery to bespoke furniture, British consumers are increasingly seeking unique, high-quality goods that offer a personal touch.

- **What Sells**: Handmade jewellery, ceramics, home décor, textiles, and leather goods are popular with British buyers. Products that tell a story or showcase local craftsmanship tend to resonate strongly, especially in artisanal markets and among tourists.

- **Where to Sell**: Artisanal products are in high demand at local markets, fairs, and festivals. Markets like **Portobello Road Market** in London or **The Shambles Market** in York provide excellent platforms for selling handcrafted goods. Online platforms like **Etsy UK** are also effective for reaching a broader audience.

Gourmet Food and Beverages

British consumers have a growing appetite for gourmet food, craft beverages, and locally sourced produce. Whether you're selling organic food, vegan products, or locally brewed craft beer, the UK's food and drink market is booming, especially for businesses that focus on sustainability and innovation.

- **What Sells**: Artisan cheeses, baked goods, craft beers, wines, chocolates, and premium snacks all perform well in the UK market. Health-conscious foods, including organic, gluten-free, and vegan options, are also in high demand. British consumers are particularly interested in locally produced and ethically sourced products.

- **Where to Sell**: Farmers' markets, food festivals, and gourmet food fairs are popular venues for selling artisanal food and drink. Notable events include **The BBC Good Food Show** and **The Great British Food Festival**. Supermarkets, delis, and online grocery platforms like **Ocado** also offer opportunities for food businesses to reach a wider market.

Beauty and Wellness Products

The UK's beauty and wellness market is rapidly expanding, with consumers increasingly prioritising skincare, cosmetics, and wellness-related products. Natural and organic beauty products, in particular, are in high demand, as consumers shift towards cleaner, more sustainable beauty routines.

- **What Sells**: Skincare, cosmetics, essential oils, and wellness-related items like yoga mats and aromatherapy products are popular in the UK. Brands that emphasise natural ingredients, sustainability, and ethical production are particularly appealing to British consumers.

- **Where to Sell**: Health and beauty products can be sold both online and at beauty and wellness fairs, such as the **Natural & Organic Products Europe** expo in London. Health food shops and wellness centres are also good retail outlets, and e-commerce platforms like **Feelunique** and **Lookfantastic** are key players in the online beauty market.

Technology and Gadgets

As a tech-savvy nation, the UK is an attractive market for innovative gadgets, electronics, and tech accessories. British consumers are eager to adopt the latest technology, especially products that offer convenience, sustainability, or a lifestyle upgrade.

- **What Sells**: Smart home devices, mobile accessories, fitness trackers, wearables, and environmentally friendly tech products are popular. With the rise of remote working, there's also growing demand for home office equipment and productivity tools.

- **Where to Sell**: Tech products are best sold online or through specialised retailers. Platforms like **Amazon UK** or tech-focused marketplaces like **Currys** are good starting points. Tech expos like **Gadget Show Live** and regional technology events are also great venues for showcasing new products.

4.2 Seasonal and Regional Trends

In addition to understanding the best-selling categories, it's important to recognise that consumer demand in the UK can vary based on the time of year and the region. Adapting your sales strategy to these trends can help you maximise your profits.

Seasonal Trends

- **Christmas Markets**: The UK has a rich tradition of Christmas markets, which are extremely popular with both locals and tourists. These markets are the perfect venue for selling festive items, including decorations, handmade gifts, winter clothing, and seasonal food and drink. Popular Christmas markets include the **Manchester Christmas Market** and the **Bath Christmas Market**.

- **Summer Festivals and Events**: The summer months see a rise in outdoor events, festivals, and markets, creating opportunities to sell products related to festivals, such as clothing, food, drinks, and crafts. Events like **Glastonbury** and **Edinburgh Festival Fringe** attract huge crowds and provide opportunities for businesses targeting festival-goers.

- **Tourism Peaks**: Tourist-heavy areas like London, Edinburgh, and the Lake District see increased foot traffic during holiday periods, particularly in the summer and over long weekends. Products that appeal to tourists, such as souvenirs, local crafts, and travel-related items, perform well during these times.

Regional Trends

- **London**: As the financial and cultural heart of the UK, London's market is dynamic and fast-paced. Consumers in London have a taste for high-end, exclusive products, and trends here tend to shift quickly. Fashion, tech, and luxury goods are particularly popular.

- **Northern England**: Cities like Manchester, Liverpool, and Leeds are known for their industrial history and creative industries. Consumers here are often drawn to trendy, innovative products that offer good value for money. Streetwear, music merchandise, and tech products resonate with the younger, urban population.

- **Scotland**: Scotland's cultural heritage and growing tech scene make it a unique market. Traditional goods, such as whisky, tartan textiles, and local food products, are popular with tourists, while cities like Edinburgh and Glasgow are hubs for tech innovation and creative industries.

- **Wales**: Wales is known for its artisanal crafts, sustainable goods, and strong local identity. Products that highlight local craftsmanship, sustainability, or natural materials are popular in both rural and urban markets, particularly in cities like Cardiff and Swansea.

4.3 Sustainability and Ethical Products

British consumers are increasingly prioritising sustainability and ethical considerations in their purchasing decisions. This trend is particularly strong among younger consumers, who are more likely to support businesses that share their values around environmental and social responsibility.

Eco-Friendly Products

Eco-conscious British consumers favour products made from sustainable materials, with minimal packaging, or that promote a zero-waste lifestyle. Whether it's fashion made from organic cotton or reusable household items, products that help reduce environmental impact are in high demand.

- **What Sells**: Reusable water bottles, bamboo toothbrushes, eco-friendly clothing, and zero-waste beauty products. Products with plastic-free or biodegradable packaging also stand out.

Ethically Sourced Goods

There is growing demand in the UK for goods that are ethically sourced, fair-trade certified, or produced under transparent and responsible working conditions. Brands that are open about their supply chains and that advocate for fair wages, good working conditions, and ethical treatment of workers often gain the trust and loyalty of British consumers.

- **What Sells**: Fair-trade food products (such as coffee, chocolate, and tea), clothing made from organic or recycled materials, and any product that supports social or environmental causes.

Chapter 4 - Summary

The UK is a diverse and dynamic market, offering countless opportunities across a wide range of product categories. Whether you're selling fashion, artisanal goods, or tech gadgets, understanding the preferences of British consumers and adapting to seasonal and regional trends can significantly boost your success. With sustainability and ethical consumption on the rise, there's also a growing market for businesses that prioritise eco-friendly, responsibly sourced products. By tapping into these trends, you can position your business to thrive in the UK.

CHAPTER 5: SELLING INDUSTRIAL PRODUCTS AND SERVICES IN THE UK

The United Kingdom is a global leader in several industrial sectors, including manufacturing, automotive, aerospace, and energy. The industrial market is diverse and driven by innovation, technology, and high standards of quality. Whether you're selling industrial machinery, engineering services, or advanced technology solutions, the UK offers vast opportunities for businesses that can meet its stringent requirements and adapt to its evolving industrial landscape.

In this chapter, we'll explore the key industrial sectors in the UK, the best strategies for entering the market, and how to navigate the regulatory environment to successfully sell industrial products and services.

5.1 Key Industrial Sectors in the UK

The UK's industrial sector is built on a foundation of innovation and advanced engineering, with key industries leading the way in both domestic production and exports. Understanding the major sectors and the opportunities they offer is crucial for targeting the right market.

Manufacturing and Engineering

- **Overview**: Manufacturing is a core part of the UK's economy, contributing significantly to exports and employing millions of people across the country. The UK is known for its high-quality manufacturing, precision engineering, and innovation in areas such as robotics, advanced materials, and automation technologies.

- **Key Regions**: The **Midlands** and the **North of England** are major manufacturing hubs, with cities like **Birmingham**, **Manchester**, and **Sheffield** leading in engineering and production. **Scotland** also has a growing manufacturing sector, particularly in renewable energy technologies.

- **Opportunities**: Companies that offer advanced manufacturing solutions, including automation, robotics, and smart factory technologies, will find demand in the UK. The **Industry 4.0** movement is gaining traction, with manufacturers looking for ways to digitise their processes and improve efficiency through data-driven solutions.

Automotive Industry

- **Overview**: The UK's automotive industry is world-renowned, producing everything from luxury cars to electric vehicles (EVs). Major brands like **Jaguar Land Rover**, **Rolls-Royce**, and **Mini** have headquarters and manufacturing plants in the UK. The government's push towards EV adoption and green transport has also spurred innovation in electric vehicle manufacturing.

- **Key Regions**: The **West Midlands**, particularly the city of **Coventry**, is the heart of the UK's automotive industry, with many major manufacturers and suppliers based here. The **North East** is also becoming a hub for EV production, with companies like **Nissan** leading the charge.

- **Opportunities**: Suppliers of automotive components, engineering services, and technology solutions related to electric vehicles and autonomous driving technologies will find growing demand. The UK is investing heavily in green transport, making it an ideal market for businesses offering EV-related products or services.

Aerospace and Defence

- **Overview**: The UK is a global leader in the aerospace and defence industries, home to major players such as **BAE Systems, Rolls-Royce** (aerospace division), and **Airbus UK**. The aerospace sector focuses on producing aircraft, satellites, and defence systems, while defence contractors play a crucial role in supplying technology to the military.

- **Key Regions**: **Bristol**, **Filton**, and **Wales** are key aerospace hubs, with facilities specialising in aircraft engineering and research. **Scotland** is also known for its contributions to space technology and satellite production.

- **Opportunities**: Businesses that supply aerospace components, engineering services, or advanced technologies will find significant opportunities in the UK. As the sector shifts towards sustainability, there is also increasing demand for lightweight materials, fuel-efficient technologies, and electric aviation solutions.

Energy and Renewable Energy

- **Overview**: The UK is a global leader in renewable energy, with a particular focus on wind power, solar energy, and nuclear energy. The **North Sea** is home to some of the largest offshore wind farms in the world, and the UK government's commitment to achieving **Net Zero** by 2050 is driving rapid growth in green energy technologies.

- **Key Regions**: **Scotland** and the **East Coast** of England are major hubs for renewable energy, particularly offshore wind. The UK also has a strong nuclear sector, with facilities in **Cumbria** and **Somerset**.

- **Opportunities**: Businesses offering renewable energy

technologies, such as wind turbines, solar panels, or energy storage systems, will find significant demand. The UK is also investing in energy efficiency and decarbonisation technologies for industrial processes, making it an attractive market for innovative solutions in this space.

Construction and Infrastructure

- **Overview**: The UK is undergoing a major infrastructure transformation, with investments in high-speed rail, green buildings, and urban development projects. The construction industry is actively seeking innovative technologies to improve sustainability, reduce carbon emissions, and increase efficiency.

- **Key Regions**: Major cities like **London**, **Birmingham**, and **Manchester** are at the forefront of urban development and infrastructure projects, including **HS2**, the UK's high-speed rail network.

- **Opportunities**: Companies that provide construction technologies, sustainable building materials, or advanced engineering services will find numerous opportunities in the UK's infrastructure sector. The government's focus on sustainability creates demand for energy-efficient and environmentally friendly construction solutions.

5.2 Entering the Industrial Market in the UK

Selling industrial products and services in the UK requires a strategic approach that combines market research, understanding procurement processes, and building strong relationships with industry stakeholders.

Market Research and Strategy Development

- **Industry Research**: Before entering the UK market, conduct thorough research on your specific industrial sector. Identify key players, competitors, and emerging trends. Understanding the local demand, regulatory environment, and procurement processes is essential for success.

- **Industry Networks**: Joining industry associations like the **Confederation of British Industry (CBI)** or attending industry trade fairs such as **Advanced Engineering** and **Subcon** can help you establish a presence and connect with key decision-makers in your sector.

Choosing the Right Distribution Model

Selecting the appropriate distribution model is critical to your success in the UK market. There are several ways to approach this, depending on your business structure and resources.

- **Direct Sales**: If you have a strong sales team, direct sales can be an effective way to build relationships with UK industrial clients. This is particularly suitable for high-value products that require customisation or technical support.

- **Local Distributors and Agents**: Many companies entering the UK market work with local distributors or agents who have established networks in the industrial sector. Distributors can help navigate the UK's complex regulatory environment and procurement processes.

- **Joint Ventures and Strategic Partnerships**: Forming partnerships with UK-based companies can give you access to local expertise, production facilities, and distribution channels. This is a good option for businesses looking to establish a long-term presence in the UK.

5.3 Navigating UK Industrial Regulations and Standards

Compliance with UK regulations and industry standards is crucial when selling industrial products and services. The UK has stringent rules regarding product quality, safety, and environmental impact, particularly in sectors like manufacturing, automotive, and energy.

Certifications and Standards

- **CE and UKCA Marking**: Many industrial products in the UK require the European Standard **CE** marking and some require **UKCA (UK Conformity Assessed)** marking, which replaced the **CE marking** after Brexit. This mark shows that products meet UK safety, health, and environmental protection standards, however it seems likely to be dropped as the CE mark has become the market standard.

- **ISO Standards**: UK industrial companies expect suppliers to adhere to **ISO standards** such as **ISO 9001** (quality management) and **ISO 14001** (environmental management). Compliance with these standards is often a prerequisite for working with UK manufacturers and government contracts.

Environmental and Safety Regulations

- **Environmental Compliance**: The UK's **Net Zero** strategy and its commitment to reducing carbon emissions have led to strict environmental regulations. Companies selling industrial products must comply with rules governing emissions, waste management, and energy efficiency.

- **Health and Safety**: The UK has strict health and safety regulations, particularly in the manufacturing and construction sectors. Compliance with the **Health and Safety at Work Act 1974** and related regulations is essential for avoiding penalties and ensuring safe working conditions.

Procurement Processes

- **Public Procurement**: If you plan to sell products or services to the public sector, you will need to navigate the UK's public procurement process. Government contracts are awarded through competitive tenders, and businesses must meet specific requirements regarding product quality, safety, and environmental standards.

- **Private Sector Procurement**: In the private sector, procurement decisions are often based on long-term relationships and the ability to deliver consistent quality. Building trust with UK industrial clients through reliability, transparency, and strong after-sales support is key to securing contracts.

5.4 Building Relationships with UK Industrial Clients

Building strong relationships with UK industrial clients is critical to success in this market. The UK places a high value on professionalism, transparency, and long-term partnerships.

Professionalism and Trust

- **Punctuality and Reliability**: UK clients expect punctuality and reliability in all business dealings. Meetings should start on time, and commitments regarding product delivery, quality, and support must be met consistently.

- **Clear Communication**: Communication in the UK tends to be formal and direct, especially in industrial sectors. Ensure that all documentation, from contracts to technical specifications, is clear and detailed.

Networking and Industry Events

- **Trade Fairs and Conferences**: Attending trade fairs and industry conferences is an excellent way to meet potential clients and showcase your products. Events like **Mach 2024** (engineering) and **Civils Expo** (construction) are key platforms for networking and building relationships in the UK industrial sector.

Tailored Solutions

UK industrial clients often seek suppliers who can offer tailored solutions. Flexibility in customising products or services to meet the specific needs of UK businesses will help you stand out in a competitive market.

Chapter 5 - Summary

The UK's industrial sector is a dynamic and innovative market, offering vast opportunities for businesses that can meet the country's high standards for quality, safety, and environmental compliance. Whether you're supplying advanced manufacturing solutions, automotive components, or renewable energy technologies, success in the UK industrial market depends on your ability to adapt to local regulations, build strong relationships, and offer tailored solutions. With the right strategy, your business can thrive in this competitive and evolving landscape.

CHAPTER 6: SELLING AT MARKETS AND FAIRS IN THE UK

The UK has a rich tradition of markets and fairs, offering a diverse range of opportunities for entrepreneurs to sell their products in person. Whether you are showcasing artisanal goods, fashion, food, or crafts, the UK's bustling markets provide direct access to a wide range of consumers, from local shoppers to tourists. Selling at these venues not only boosts your brand's visibility but also allows you to build personal relationships with your customers, gather feedback, and test new products.

In this chapter, we will explore how to get started with selling at markets and fairs, provide an overview of the UK's most famous markets, and offer tips on how to maximise your sales with effective stall design and customer engagement.

6.1 Famous Markets in the UK

The UK is home to some of the most famous and historic markets in the world. From London's eclectic street markets to traditional farmers' markets in rural areas, there are countless opportunities to find the right venue for your products.

Borough Market (London)

- **Overview**: Located in the heart of London, **Borough Market** is one of the capital's most iconic food markets. It specialises in gourmet food, organic produce, and artisanal products. The market attracts both locals and tourists, making it an ideal place to sell high-quality food and drink items.

- **What Sells**: Organic produce, artisan cheese, baked goods, craft beverages, and speciality foods from around the world.

Camden Market (London)

- **Overview**: **Camden Market** is known for its vibrant, alternative atmosphere and is a hub for fashion, vintage clothing, jewellery, crafts, and art. The market is particularly popular with young, trendy shoppers and tourists looking for unique, edgy items.
- **What Sells**: Streetwear, handmade jewellery, vintage fashion, custom art, and quirky home décor.

Manchester Christmas Market

- **Overview**: Held annually in the heart of Manchester, the **Manchester Christmas Market** is one of the UK's most popular festive markets. The market spreads across several city-centre locations and attracts thousands of visitors looking for Christmas gifts, seasonal food, and festive decorations.
- **What Sells**: Handcrafted gifts, festive decorations, winter clothing, gourmet food and drink, and traditional Christmas goods.

The Shambles Market (York)

- **Overview**: The **Shambles Market** in York is a historic market set in the medieval streets of one of the UK's most picturesque cities. It offers a variety of stalls selling local food, crafts, and artisan products. The market is popular with both locals and tourists, particularly those looking for traditional and unique products.
- **What Sells**: Handmade crafts, home décor, local food and drink, and bespoke gifts.

Portobello Road Market (London)

- **Overview**: Famous for its antiques, **Portobello Road Market** in Notting Hill is a must-visit for collectors and tourists alike. It also hosts stalls selling fashion, art, and food, making it one of the most diverse and well-known markets in London.

- **What Sells**: Antiques, vintage goods, artwork, fashion, jewellery, and street food.

6.2 Setting Up Your Stall

A well-designed and organised stall is crucial to attracting customers and maximising sales. The appearance of your stall is often the first impression customers will have of your business, so it's important to make it inviting, professional, and visually appealing.

Stall Design and Layout

- **Keep It Open and Accessible**: Make sure your stall is easy for customers to approach. Avoid cluttering the front of the stall with too many products or displays, which can create a barrier. Keep pathways clear and ensure that products are neatly displayed so that customers can browse comfortably.

- **Use Eye-Catching Displays**: Visual appeal is key when it comes to drawing in customers. Use height and variation in your displays to create an interesting visual flow. For example, place key products at eye level, and use props or stands to elevate products for better visibility. Bright, colourful signage that clearly displays your brand name and product offerings can also help attract attention.

- **Branding and Signage**: Make sure your stall reflects your brand's identity. Use cohesive colours, fonts, and logos on your signage, business cards, and packaging. Display your business name prominently and consider including a brief description of what makes your products special (e.g., "Handmade in Wales" or "Eco-Friendly Designs").

- **Lighting**: If the market or fair runs into the evening or is indoors, good lighting can make a big difference. Use soft, warm lighting to highlight your products and create a welcoming atmosphere.

Transporting and Displaying Your Goods

- **Portability**: Ensure your stall setup is easy to transport and assemble. Pop-up gazebos, foldable tables, and lightweight display racks can make setting up quick and hassle-free. Invest in sturdy packaging for transporting delicate items and ensure you have enough stock to last the entire day.

- **Display Materials**: Use high-quality materials like wood, metal, or cloth for your displays to enhance the aesthetic of your stall. Avoid using too much plastic, which can look cheap and detract from the quality of your products.

6.3 Connecting with Customers

One of the key advantages of selling at markets and fairs is the opportunity to engage directly with customers. Building a personal connection can make all the difference, leading to immediate sales and long-term customer loyalty.

Engagement and Customer Interaction

- **Be Approachable**: Smile and make eye contact with passersby, but avoid being overly pushy. Greet customers warmly and allow them to browse without feeling pressured. Being approachable and available for questions is often enough to encourage interest and conversation.

- **Storytelling**: Customers love to know the story behind what they're buying. Whether you're selling handmade jewellery or artisanal food, share the story of your products. Explain the materials, the craftsmanship, or the inspiration behind your creations. This can build an emotional connection with the customer and increase the perceived value of your products.

. **Offer Samples**: If you're selling food or beauty products, offering samples is a great way to engage customers. Free samples encourage people to try your products and give you the opportunity to interact with them. Just be mindful of market rules and food safety regulations.

Encouraging Sales and Repeat Customers

. **Discounts and Special Offers**: Offering special discounts or deals can help boost sales, especially towards the end of the market day. Consider offering "buy one, get one free" deals, discounts for purchasing multiple items, or a small gift with purchase to encourage sales.

. **Business Cards and Follow-Ups**: Always have business cards or leaflets available so customers can find you again, either at future markets or online. Encourage them to follow your social media pages or sign up for your email list to keep them updated on new products or market appearances.

. **Loyalty Programmes**: Consider offering a simple loyalty programme, such as a stamp card where customers can earn a discount after making several purchases. This can encourage repeat business and foster long-term relationships.

6.4 Navigating Market Regulations and Costs

Before setting up at any market or fair, it's essential to understand the regulations, costs, and requirements for vendors. Each market has its own rules, so it's important to check with the market organisers beforehand.

Applying for a Stall

- **Market Research**: Not all markets are created equal, so it's important to research the markets and fairs that are the best fit for your products. Visit potential markets in person if possible to get a feel for the customer base and the types of products sold.

- **Application Process**: Most markets require vendors to apply for a stall in advance, providing details about the types of products they sell and any necessary certifications. This can be done through the market's website or by contacting the organisers directly. Applications for seasonal or high-traffic markets, like Christmas markets, often need to be submitted several months in advance.

- **Vendor Fees**: Stall fees can vary significantly depending on the market's size, location, and popularity. Smaller local markets might charge a nominal fee, while larger city or Christmas markets can have higher fees. Some markets may also require vendors to share a percentage of their sales.

Insurance and Licensing

- **Public Liability Insurance**: Most markets will require you to have public liability insurance, which covers you in case of accidents or injuries that occur at your stall. It's essential to have this insurance in place before attending any markets, and you may be asked to provide proof of cover.

- **Food Hygiene and Safety**: If you're selling food, you'll need to comply with UK food hygiene regulations and have the appropriate licences in place. The **Food Standards Agency (FSA)** regulates food safety, and you may be required to have your business inspected before you can sell at markets.

Chapter 6 - Summary

Selling at markets and fairs is a fantastic way to connect with customers, build your brand, and generate sales in a lively, dynamic environment. By setting up an attractive and accessible stall, engaging directly with customers, and understanding market regulations, you can make the most of the UK's vibrant market scene. Whether you're selling artisanal crafts, gourmet food, or fashion, markets and fairs offer invaluable opportunities to grow your business and reach a wide audience.

CHAPTER 7: SELLING ONLINE IN THE UK

The UK is one of the largest and most dynamic e-commerce markets in Europe, with consumers increasingly turning to online platforms for convenience, variety, and competitive pricing. Whether you're a small business owner selling artisanal goods or a larger enterprise offering technology products, having an online presence is essential for reaching UK consumers. In this chapter, we will explore the key steps to setting up an online store, optimising it for British consumers, and managing payments, shipping, and customer service in the UK's fast-paced e-commerce environment.

7.1 Popular E-Commerce Platforms in the UK

There are several e-commerce platforms that cater to different types of businesses, each with its own strengths and features. Choosing the right platform for your products is the first step to building a successful online store.

Amazon UK

Amazon UK is the largest online marketplace in the country and is a powerful platform for businesses looking to reach a broad audience. Amazon provides sellers with a well-established infrastructure, including logistics, marketing tools, and access to millions of UK consumers.

- **Advantages**: Access to a massive customer base, trusted by consumers, comprehensive shipping and fulfilment services via **Fulfilment by Amazon (FBA)**.
- **Disadvantages**: High competition, fees can be

significant, and businesses must adhere to Amazon's rules and policies.

- **Best for**: Sellers looking to scale quickly, particularly those offering consumer goods, electronics, and popular retail items.

Etsy UK

Etsy is the go-to platform for independent sellers offering handmade, vintage, or unique products. Etsy is popular in the UK for artisan products, crafts, and bespoke items, and it provides a marketplace where businesses can reach a targeted audience of consumers who value creativity and craftsmanship.

- **Advantages**: Ideal for niche products, strong community of buyers looking for handmade or vintage items, relatively low fees compared to other platforms.
- **Disadvantages**: Limited for businesses selling mass-produced items, smaller customer base than platforms like Amazon.
- **Best for**: Small businesses selling handmade jewellery, crafts, home décor, vintage clothing, or personalised gifts.

eBay UK

eBay UK is one of the most well-established online marketplaces, offering a platform for both new and used goods. With a wide customer base, eBay is ideal for sellers who want flexibility in pricing, including the option to use auctions or fixed prices.

- **Advantages**: Versatile platform that allows for auction-style sales and fixed prices, well-established with a large UK customer base.
- **Disadvantages**: High competition, sellers must manage their own fulfilment unless using **eBay's Global Shipping Programme**.
- **Best for**: Sellers offering both new and second-hand items, including fashion, electronics, collectibles, and

automotive parts.

Shopify

If you want to set up your own branded online store, **Shopify** is one of the best platforms for creating a professional-looking e-commerce site. It provides customisable templates, payment integration, and marketing tools that help you build your online brand without relying on third-party marketplaces.

- **Advantages**: Fully customisable, no direct competition from other sellers, comprehensive payment and shipping integrations.

- **Disadvantages**: Requires more effort to drive traffic to your site, costs can be higher due to monthly subscription fees and additional app integrations.

- **Best for**: Businesses looking to build a unique online store with full control over branding and customer experience.

7.2 Crafting a Localised Marketing Strategy

Once your online store is set up, it's essential to tailor your marketing strategy to resonate with British consumers. From localising your website's language to understanding the buying habits of UK shoppers, a well-thought-out approach will help you stand out in the competitive UK e-commerce market.

Website Localisation and SEO

To ensure your online store appeals to UK consumers, your website should be fully localised. This includes using UK English spelling, displaying prices in **pounds sterling (£)**, and providing shipping options that are relevant to British buyers.

- **UK English**: Small details like using "colour" instead of "color" or "favourite" instead of "favorite" can make your website feel more familiar and trustworthy to UK consumers.

- **UK-Specific Content**: Make sure that product

descriptions, blog content, and any promotional material are tailored to UK preferences and trends.

- **SEO (Search Engine Optimisation)**: Optimise your website for **Google UK** by using location-specific keywords and phrases that are commonly searched by UK consumers. Use tools like **Google Keyword Planner** to identify popular search terms in the UK market.

Social Media Marketing

Social media is a key driver of online sales in the UK, with platforms like **Instagram**, **Facebook**, and **TikTok** playing a major role in product discovery and consumer engagement.

- **Instagram**: Instagram is particularly popular for fashion, beauty, and lifestyle products. Use visually appealing content to showcase your products, and consider using **Instagram Shopping** to allow users to purchase directly through the platform.

- **Facebook Ads**: **Facebook** remains one of the best platforms for targeted advertising, allowing you to reach specific demographics based on location, interests, and purchasing behaviour.

- **TikTok**: **TikTok** has become a powerful platform for product discovery, particularly among younger consumers. Creating engaging, short-form videos that showcase your products or tell your brand's story can help you tap into this growing audience.

Email Marketing

Email marketing is a powerful tool for keeping customers engaged and driving repeat purchases. By sending regular newsletters, promotional offers, or personalised product recommendations, you can encourage customers to return to your site.

- **Personalised Offers**: British consumers respond well

to personalised recommendations and offers. Use customer data to send targeted emails, such as product suggestions based on past purchases or discounts on items they've shown interest in.

- **Seasonal Campaigns**: Build email campaigns around key shopping periods in the UK, such as **Christmas**, **Black Friday**, and **Easter**. Highlight any special promotions or seasonal products to encourage sales.

7.3 Payment Methods and Secure Transactions

UK consumers expect a variety of payment options when shopping online, and ensuring that your website supports their preferred methods is crucial to building trust and securing sales.

Popular Payment Methods in the UK

- **Credit and Debit Cards**: The most common payment method in the UK is credit and debit cards, including **Visa**, **Mastercard**, and **American Express**. Ensure your site supports secure card payments with **SSL encryption** to protect customer data.

- **PayPal**: **PayPal** is widely trusted by UK consumers and is a popular payment option, particularly for online transactions. Offering PayPal as a payment method can increase customer confidence in your store.

- **Apple Pay and Google Pay**: Mobile payment options like **Apple Pay** and **Google Pay** are growing in popularity, particularly among younger consumers. Ensure your site supports these contactless payment methods to cater to tech-savvy shoppers.

Secure Transactions and Trust Signals

UK consumers are increasingly concerned about online security, so it's important to build trust through secure payment systems and clear communication.

- **SSL Certificates**: Make sure your website has an **SSL certificate** (indicated by the padlock symbol in the browser's address bar) to encrypt data and protect customer information during transactions.

- **Trust Badges**: Displaying trust badges, such as **PayPal Verified**, **Norton Secured**, or **Trustpilot**, can reassure customers that your website is safe and reliable.

7.4 Shipping and Logistics for UK Consumers

Fast, affordable, and reliable shipping is a key factor in satisfying UK consumers. Offering multiple shipping options and ensuring that your logistics run smoothly can enhance your customer experience and help you stand out from competitors.

Domestic Shipping Solutions

- **Royal Mail**: The UK's national postal service, **Royal Mail**, is a reliable and cost-effective option for domestic shipping. It offers a range of services, including **1st Class**, **2nd Class**, and **Tracked & Signed** options, which are ideal for small businesses.

- **Private Couriers**: For larger orders or time-sensitive deliveries, private couriers like **DHL**, **DPD**, and **Hermes** provide fast, reliable service across the UK. They offer next-day and even same-day delivery options, which can be a strong selling point for your customers.

Free and Fast Delivery Expectations

UK consumers are used to fast shipping options, especially with platforms like **Amazon Prime** offering next-day or same-day delivery. While it may not always be feasible for small businesses to offer such quick shipping, providing options like **express delivery** or **free delivery on orders over a certain amount** can help you compete.

- **Click-and-Collect**: Many UK consumers also prefer **click-and-collect** services, where they can purchase online and pick up their items from a nearby store or collection point. If possible, offering this service can attract customers who want to avoid shipping costs or delivery delays.

Returns and Customer Service

- **Flexible Return Policies**: UK consumers expect hassle-free returns, especially for online purchases. Offering a flexible return policy, such as free returns within 30 days, can build customer trust and encourage them to buy with confidence.

- **Clear Communication**: Ensure that your shipping and returns policies are clearly stated on your website, including details on how to return items, expected delivery times, and any associated costs.

7.5 Managing Customer Service for E-Commerce

Providing excellent customer service is essential for building trust and loyalty in the online marketplace. In the UK, customers expect responsive and helpful service, whether they're enquiring about a product, checking the status of an order, or requesting a return.

Customer Support Channels

- **Live Chat**: Many online shoppers prefer the convenience of live chat, allowing them to get instant answers to their questions. Implementing a live chat feature on your website can improve customer satisfaction and help convert potential buyers.

- **Email and Phone Support**: Offering both email and phone support gives customers flexibility in how they reach out to you. Respond to emails promptly, ideally within 24 hours, and ensure that phone support is available during business hours in the UK time zone.

Handling Complaints and Feedback

- **Timely Responses**: UK customers value timely responses to complaints or issues. If a customer raises a concern, respond quickly and offer a clear resolution, whether that's a replacement, refund, or store credit.

- **Encourage Reviews**: Positive reviews can significantly boost your credibility in the UK market. Encourage satisfied customers to leave reviews on platforms like **Trustpilot**, **Google Reviews**, or directly on your website. Responding to reviews, both positive and negative, shows that you value customer feedback.

Chapter 7 - Summary

Selling online in the UK offers vast opportunities, but success requires careful attention to the details of your e-commerce setup, marketing strategy, and customer service. By choosing the right platform, localising your website and marketing efforts, offering secure payment options, and providing excellent shipping and support, you can build a thriving online business that resonates with UK consumers. With e-commerce continuing to grow rapidly, ensuring your business stands out through reliability, customer engagement, and trust is essential to long-term success.

CHAPTER 8: MARKETING STRATEGIES FOR UK CONSUMERS

Marketing in the United Kingdom is a unique mix of traditional values and digital innovation. UK consumers are sophisticated, and their buying decisions are often influenced by price, quality, ethics, and brand reputation. To succeed in this competitive market, you need to understand the preferences of British consumers and the best channels to reach them. In this chapter, we'll explore the most effective marketing strategies for UK businesses, including digital advertising, social media engagement, influencer marketing, and more traditional methods like print and outdoor advertising.

8.1 Understanding UK Buyer Behaviour

Before you begin developing your marketing strategy, it's crucial to understand how UK consumers think, shop, and make purchasing decisions. British consumers are typically well-informed, price-conscious, and increasingly focused on sustainability and ethics.

Price Sensitivity and Value for Money

British consumers are often price-conscious, especially in the current economic climate. They expect value for their money, but they are also willing to spend more on products that demonstrate high quality or offer additional benefits, such as sustainability or ethical production.

- **Discounts and Offers**: Offering discounts, bundle deals, or free shipping on larger orders can be an effective way to attract cost-conscious shoppers. Many UK consumers are swayed by special promotions or limited-time offers, especially if they believe they're getting a good deal.

- **Quality and Longevity**: While price is important, British consumers value products that offer long-term value. Emphasise the quality, durability, and craftsmanship of your products to justify higher prices and attract those willing to invest in better goods.

Sustainability and Ethics

There's a growing demand for sustainable and ethically produced goods in the UK. Consumers, particularly younger buyers, are increasingly concerned about the environmental impact of their purchases and the ethical practices behind them.

- **Transparency**: Be transparent about your supply chain, materials, and manufacturing processes. British consumers appreciate brands that are upfront about their efforts to reduce environmental impact and support ethical practices.

- **Green Marketing**: Incorporate sustainability into your marketing campaigns. Highlight eco-friendly materials, ethical sourcing, and any certifications (e.g., Fair Trade, Organic) your products have.

Brand Loyalty and Trust

UK consumers tend to be loyal to brands they trust. Building trust takes time, but once a relationship is established, British buyers are likely to remain loyal, especially if they feel your brand aligns with their values.

- **Customer Service**: Provide excellent customer service and be responsive to feedback. Positive interactions build trust and encourage long-term customer loyalty.

- **Reviews and Testimonials**: Encourage satisfied customers to leave reviews, as British consumers often rely on reviews and recommendations when making purchase decisions. Displaying customer testimonials or Trustpilot reviews on your website can help build credibility.

8.2 Digital Marketing Channels

Digital marketing is one of the most effective ways to reach UK consumers. Whether through social media, search engines, or email campaigns, having a strong digital presence is essential for driving traffic and conversions.

Search Engine Optimisation (SEO)

Optimising your website for search engines like **Google UK** is crucial for attracting organic traffic. UK consumers often use search engines to research products before making a purchase, so appearing at the top of search results can significantly boost your visibility.

- **Local SEO**: If you have a physical presence in the UK or want to attract local customers, focus on local SEO. Use location-based keywords and ensure your business is listed on **Google My Business** to appear in local search results.
- **Keyword Research**: Tailor your website content to include UK-specific search terms. Tools like **Google Keyword Planner** can help you identify popular search terms in the UK that relate to your products.

Google Ads

Google Ads is one of the most effective ways to target UK consumers with pay-per-click (PPC) advertising. You can run targeted ad campaigns that reach your audience based on their search queries, demographics, and location.

- **Search Ads**: Appear at the top of Google search results when users search for keywords related to your products. This is especially useful for capturing consumers who are ready to buy.

- **Display Ads**: Use visual banner ads on relevant websites to increase brand awareness and drive traffic to your site.

Social Media Marketing

Social media is a key component of digital marketing in the UK, particularly on platforms like **Instagram, Facebook, TikTok**, and **Twitter**. Each platform caters to different demographics, so it's essential to tailor your content to suit your target audience.

- **Instagram**: Particularly popular for fashion, beauty, and lifestyle brands, Instagram is a visual platform where you can showcase your products through high-quality images and engaging stories. Use **Instagram Shopping** to allow users to purchase products directly through the app.

- **Facebook**: Facebook's advanced targeting tools make it an ideal platform for running ads to specific demographics. You can target users based on their location, age, interests, and purchasing behaviour, making it a powerful tool for both brand awareness and direct sales.

- **TikTok**: As one of the fastest-growing platforms in the UK, TikTok is ideal for brands targeting younger audiences. Short, engaging videos that showcase your products or brand story can go viral and significantly boost visibility.

- **Twitter**: Twitter is a great platform for real-time interaction with your audience. Use it to share news, promotions, and engage with consumers directly. It's particularly effective for customer service and brand engagement.

Email Marketing

Email marketing remains one of the most cost-effective ways

to engage with UK consumers. By sending regular newsletters, personalised offers, and product updates, you can keep your audience engaged and encourage repeat purchases.

- **Personalisation**: Personalised emails that address customers by name and recommend products based on their past behaviour tend to perform better. Use customer data to tailor your email content to individual preferences.

- **Automated Campaigns**: Set up automated email sequences for new subscribers, abandoned carts, or post-purchase follow-ups. Automation allows you to stay in touch with your customers without manually sending each email.

8.3 Influencer Marketing in the UK

Influencer marketing has become a powerful tool in the UK, particularly for fashion, beauty, and lifestyle brands. Collaborating with influencers allows you to reach new audiences, build brand awareness, and drive sales through authentic recommendations.

Choosing the Right Influencers

Not all influencers are created equal, so it's important to choose influencers whose audience aligns with your target market. UK consumers are savvy and can quickly spot inauthentic partnerships, so make sure the influencer's values and content are a good fit for your brand.

- **Micro-Influencers**: These influencers have smaller followings (typically 5,000–50,000 followers) but often have highly engaged audiences. They are ideal for brands looking to build trust and reach niche markets without a huge budget.

- **Macro-Influencers**: With larger followings (50,000+), macro-influencers can help increase brand awareness on a broader scale. They're a good option for established brands looking to expand their reach quickly, but they often come with higher costs.

Influencer Campaigns

- **Product Reviews**: Send products to influencers for them to review and share with their audience. Authentic, positive reviews can significantly boost sales, especially when the influencer demonstrates how your product fits into their daily life.

- **Sponsored Posts**: Pay influencers to create sponsored posts featuring your products. This could be a single post, a series of stories, or a dedicated video.

- **Affiliate Marketing**: Offer influencers a commission for every sale they generate. This encourages them to actively promote your products and drive traffic to your site.

8.4 Traditional Marketing Methods

While digital marketing is dominant, traditional marketing methods like print advertising, outdoor advertising, and direct mail can still be effective for reaching certain UK demographics, especially older consumers or those in more rural areas.

Print Advertising

Print advertising in magazines, newspapers, or brochures can help build credibility and reach consumers who prefer more traditional media. Regional newspapers or niche magazines are ideal for targeting specific audiences or promoting local products.

- **Best for**: Niche markets, luxury products, and targeting local communities.

Outdoor Advertising

Billboards, bus stop ads, and posters are effective ways to reach a broad audience, particularly in busy urban areas. Outdoor advertising is ideal for promoting seasonal sales or driving brand awareness.

- **Best for**: Brands looking to increase visibility, particularly in city centres or high-traffic locations.

Direct Mail

Although direct mail may seem outdated, it can be a highly effective way to engage with UK consumers, especially for local businesses. Sending out catalogues, postcards, or special offers directly to potential customers' homes can create a personal connection and encourage them to visit your online or physical store.

- **Best for**: Small businesses targeting local communities or offering exclusive deals to specific demographics.

Chapter 8 - Summary

To successfully market your products in the UK, you need to take a multi-channel approach that combines digital innovation with an understanding of British consumer behaviour. By leveraging the power of social media, influencer marketing, and email campaigns, while also considering traditional methods like print and outdoor advertising, you can reach a diverse audience and build long-term customer loyalty. Tailoring your marketing efforts to the UK's preferences—especially focusing on value, quality, and sustainability—will help you stand out in a competitive market.

CHAPTER 9: NAVIGATING UK BUSINESS ETIQUETTE

When doing business in the United Kingdom, understanding and respecting British business etiquette is essential to building successful relationships with clients, partners, and customers. The UK business environment values professionalism, punctuality, and politeness, but it is also shaped by a balance of tradition and modernity. Whether you're attending formal meetings in London's financial district or networking at industry events in Manchester, knowing how to navigate British business culture will give you an edge in establishing rapport and trust.

In this chapter, we'll explore the key aspects of UK business etiquette, including communication styles, meeting conduct, dress codes, and how to build long-term business relationships.

9.1 Formality and Politeness in Business Interactions

British business culture tends to be formal, especially in initial meetings, but it also values politeness and understated professionalism. While there are variations across industries and regions, being polite, respectful, and avoiding overly aggressive sales tactics is crucial.

Addressing Colleagues and Clients

- **Titles and Last Names**: When first meeting someone in a professional setting, it's best to address them using their title (e.g., Mr, Mrs, Dr) and last name. Only switch to first names when invited to do so, as British professionals often prefer to maintain a level of formality, especially in the beginning.

- **Politeness**: Always use polite language, such as "please," "thank you," and "excuse me." Avoid interrupting during conversations, as this is considered impolite. Active listening and measured responses are highly valued in British business culture.

- **Small Talk**: British professionals often engage in small talk before diving into business discussions. Topics like the weather, sports (particularly football and rugby), or travel are safe choices. However, avoid topics like politics or personal matters unless you know the person well.

Emails and Written Communication

- **Professional Tone**: Written communication in the UK should maintain a formal and polite tone, particularly in emails. Start with "Dear [Title and Last Name]" and use "Yours sincerely" or "Kind regards" to close. Avoid using slang or overly casual language, especially when addressing new contacts or clients.

- **Be Clear and Concise**: British professionals appreciate clarity and efficiency. Keep your emails and documents clear, concise, and to the point. Avoid being overly wordy, and ensure that your communication is well-structured and easy to follow.

9.2 Business Meetings and Networking

Meetings and networking events in the UK can vary in style, depending on the industry, but certain rules around punctuality, professionalism, and meeting conduct are universally respected. Knowing how to behave in these settings will help you leave a positive impression.

Punctuality

- **Arriving on Time**: Punctuality is highly valued in UK business culture. Always aim to arrive for meetings a few minutes early, as being late is considered unprofessional. If you are delayed, be sure to notify your host in advance with an explanation and an expected time of arrival.

Meeting Conduct

- **Structure and Formality**: Business meetings in the UK are typically structured and follow an agenda. Be prepared with relevant data, documentation, or presentations, and ensure that you stick to the meeting's objectives. Small talk at the beginning is common, but once the meeting starts, it tends to be focused and formal.

- **Active Participation**: While it's important to contribute, avoid dominating the conversation or interrupting others. British business culture values balance and collaboration, so allow everyone to have their say. Make your points clearly and concisely, and be prepared to answer questions with facts or data.

- **Decision-Making**: British decision-making processes can sometimes be slower than in other cultures, as they tend to be consensus-driven. Don't be surprised if there's a need for follow-up meetings before final decisions are made, particularly in larger organisations. Patience and thoroughness are key.

Networking Events

- **Business Cards**: Exchanging business cards is a common practice in the UK, but it is usually done towards the end of a meeting or networking conversation. Present your card with both hands, and be sure to carefully receive the other person's card as a sign of respect.

- **Networking Etiquette**: Networking events in the UK can range from formal receptions to more relaxed gatherings. Regardless of the setting, remain polite, approachable, and professional. Avoid hard-sell tactics; instead, focus on building relationships and establishing rapport.

- **Follow-Ups**: After meetings or networking events, it's customary to follow up with a thank-you email or message. Recap the main points discussed and, if appropriate, outline the next steps or actions to maintain momentum in the business relationship.

9.3 Dress Codes in UK Business Settings

Dress codes in the UK vary by industry and region, but business attire generally leans towards conservative and professional. Whether you're meeting with corporate clients in London or attending a creative industry event in Manchester, dressing appropriately for the occasion is essential.

Formal Business Attire

- **Suits for Men**: In most corporate settings, especially in industries like finance, law, and consultancy, men are expected to wear a dark-coloured suit (navy or charcoal are the most common) with a tie. Shoes should be polished, and accessories like belts and watches should be understated.

- **Business Dress for Women**: For women, a tailored business suit (either with trousers or a skirt) or a conservative dress is typically expected in formal settings. Neutral or dark colours are preferred, and accessories should be professional and not overly flashy.

Business Casual

- **Creative and Tech Industries**: In sectors such as tech, media, and creative industries, the dress code is often more relaxed, with **business casual** attire being acceptable. For men, this might mean a shirt without a tie and smart trousers, while women might wear a blouse with a skirt or smart trousers.

- **Smart Casual for Networking**: At networking events,

especially those that are more informal or outside of traditional corporate environments, **smart casual** attire is appropriate. This could include a smart jacket with jeans for men or a blouse with smart trousers or a skirt for women. Always err on the side of caution and dress slightly more formally if unsure.

Regional Variations

- **London**: In London, the dress code tends to be more formal, particularly in corporate environments like banking or law. If you're attending a meeting or event in the City of London (the financial district), stick to business formal attire unless otherwise specified.

- **Other Regions**: Outside of London, the dress code can be more relaxed. In cities like Manchester, Birmingham, or Edinburgh, business casual is more common, especially in creative or tech sectors. However, it's always advisable to confirm the expected dress code in advance.

9.4 Building Long-Term Business Relationships

Establishing trust and building long-term relationships is key to success in the UK business world. British professionals tend to prefer working with partners they know well, and fostering a relationship based on mutual respect and reliability can lead to long-term partnerships.

Consistency and Reliability

- **Deliver on Promises**: UK businesses value reliability and consistency. Once you've agreed on a deal or project, it's crucial to follow through on your promises and meet deadlines. Failing to deliver can quickly damage your reputation and the relationship.

- **Under-Promise, Over-Deliver**: A common practice in UK business culture is to under-promise and over-deliver. Rather than making bold claims, focus on delivering high-quality results that exceed expectations. This approach helps build credibility and trust over time.

Patience and Persistence

- **Longer Decision-Making**: The decision-making process in the UK can be slower compared to other business cultures, as companies often seek consensus and prefer to thoroughly evaluate options before committing. Be patient, and avoid applying too much pressure during negotiations.

- **Follow-Up**: British businesspeople appreciate follow-up and attention to detail. After meetings or completing a project, check in to ensure the client is satisfied and address any concerns they may have. This helps strengthen the relationship and shows that you value their business.

Socialising and Building Rapport

- **Business Meals**: While much of UK business is conducted in the office, social events like business lunches or dinners are common. These meals are a good opportunity to build rapport in a more relaxed setting. However, avoid discussing business matters too early in the meal—start with light conversation and ease into business topics later on.

- **Sports and Events**: For some industries, particularly finance and law, attending sporting events (such as football or rugby matches) or cultural events (such as theatre) is a way to strengthen business relationships. If invited, attending such events shows your willingness to engage socially, which can help cement a business relationship.

Chapter 9 - Summary

Navigating UK business etiquette involves a blend of formality, politeness, and professionalism. By understanding the importance of clear communication, punctuality, and appropriate dress codes, you can build strong, respectful relationships with British colleagues and clients. Building long-term partnerships requires consistency, patience, and the ability to deliver on promises. As you deepen your connections in the UK business world, these small cultural considerations will help you stand out as a reliable and professional partner, opening doors to lasting business success.

CHAPTER 10: CONCLUSION – UNLOCKING SUCCESS IN THE UK

The United Kingdom offers a diverse, vibrant, and ever-evolving market for entrepreneurs, whether you're selling artisanal crafts at local markets, industrial products to major corporations, or cutting-edge technology online. Succeeding in the UK requires more than just great products and services—it demands an understanding of British consumer behaviour, a mastery of the country's business etiquette, and the ability to navigate the complexities of its regulatory landscape.

In this final chapter, we'll summarise the key takeaways from the guide and outline the critical steps you need to take to unlock long-term success in the UK.

10.1 Key Takeaways for Travelling and Selling in the UK

Over the course of this guide, we've explored various aspects of travelling, selling, and doing business in the UK. Here are the most important points to keep in mind as you take the next steps with your business.

Understanding the UK's Geography and Culture

- The UK is made up of four distinct nations—England, Scotland, Wales, and Northern Ireland—each with its own unique cultural identity and consumer preferences. Understanding these regional differences will help you tailor your approach and connect more effectively with local markets.

- British consumers are generally price-conscious but place great value on quality, ethical sourcing, and sustainability. They are also increasingly favouring local and eco-friendly products, so consider how your offerings can align with these values.

Navigating the UK's Transport and Logistics

- Travelling within the UK is convenient, thanks to its well-developed transport infrastructure. Trains, buses, and motorways make it easy to reach urban and rural markets alike. Efficient transport is crucial for attending markets, fulfilling orders, and delivering goods on time.

- Make sure your business is prepared for the logistics of managing inventory, transporting goods, and shipping products to customers across the UK. Reliable shipping and offering convenient delivery options, such as click-and-collect, are essential for success in both physical and online sales.

Setting Up and Growing Your Business in the UK

- Choosing the right business structure—whether as a sole trader, limited company, or partnership—will impact how you manage taxes, liabilities, and day-to-day operations. Ensure that you register with the appropriate authorities and comply with UK tax regulations, including VAT if necessary.

- Adapting to UK consumer protection laws, such as offering clear returns policies and ensuring product safety, is vital to maintaining trust and credibility with British consumers. Good customer service and transparent practices will help you build a loyal customer base.

Leveraging the Power of Markets, Fairs, and E-Commerce

- Markets and fairs are a great way to engage directly with consumers, particularly for artisanal products, fashion, and food. Choose the right venues, design your stall to attract attention, and engage with customers to build relationships and encourage repeat business.

- In today's digital landscape, having an online presence is essential. Whether through a marketplace like Amazon or Etsy, or your own website, ensure that your online store is optimised for UK consumers. Offer secure payment options, clear shipping policies, and excellent customer service to build trust and drive sales.

Effective Marketing Strategies for UK Consumers

- Understanding UK buyer behaviour is key to crafting an effective marketing strategy. British consumers value quality and ethical production, but they are also highly responsive to value for money and special offers.

- Leverage digital marketing channels such as search engine optimisation (SEO), social media, and email marketing to reach your target audience. Platforms like Instagram, Facebook, and Google Ads offer powerful tools for reaching British consumers, while influencer marketing can help build brand awareness and trust.

- Traditional marketing methods, including print advertising and outdoor ads, can still play an important role, especially when targeting local communities or specific demographics.

Navigating Business Etiquette and Building Relationships

- British business culture is professional, polite, and often formal, especially in the initial stages of building relationships. Punctuality, politeness, and clear communication are highly valued.

- Building long-term business relationships in the UK requires patience, reliability, and consistency. Follow through on promises, deliver high-quality products or services, and stay attentive to customer needs to foster trust and loyalty.

- Networking and attending industry events can provide valuable opportunities to connect with potential clients, partners, and suppliers, helping to expand your business and establish your reputation in the UK.

10.2 Steps to Unlocking Success in the UK

To summarise, here are the critical steps you should take to ensure your business thrives in the UK market:

1. Research and Understand Your Target Market

- Spend time researching the regions and consumer segments you plan to target. Understand local preferences, spending habits, and cultural nuances to effectively position your products.
- Keep up to date with current trends in sustainability, ethical consumption, and technology, as these are major drivers in UK consumer behaviour.

2. Establish a Strong Business Foundation

- Choose the right business structure and ensure compliance with all legal and tax obligations. Proper registration and adherence to UK regulations are critical to operating smoothly in the UK market.
- Focus on building a strong brand identity that resonates with UK consumers, particularly in areas like quality, sustainability, and ethical practices.

3. Build an Effective Sales Strategy

- Take advantage of both offline and online sales channels. Attend markets and fairs to engage directly with customers, while also building a robust e-commerce presence to reach a wider audience.
- Consider offering a mix of traditional and digital payment methods, and make sure your logistics are

optimised for quick, efficient deliveries.

4. Tailor Your Marketing to the UK

- Develop a localised marketing strategy that speaks to British consumers' values and interests. Use a combination of SEO, social media, email marketing, and traditional advertising to build brand awareness and drive sales.

- Consider working with UK influencers or engaging with local communities to increase visibility and establish trust with your target audience.

5. Build Strong Business Relationships

- Be patient and persistent when building business relationships in the UK. Invest time in networking, attending industry events, and following up with potential clients or partners.

- Focus on long-term relationships based on trust, professionalism, and reliability. Deliver consistently on promises to build your reputation and secure repeat business.

Final Thoughts: Unlocking Your Potential in the UK

The UK offers a wealth of opportunities for businesses, from bustling urban centres like London and Manchester to the charming markets of rural Wales and Scotland. The country's dynamic consumer market, combined with its openness to innovation and ethical business practices, makes it an attractive destination for entrepreneurs.

By combining an understanding of the UK's cultural and regional diversity with a strategic approach to marketing, logistics, and business etiquette, you can unlock the full potential of this unique market. Whether you are selling locally made goods at a street market or launching a cutting-edge tech product online, the

UK rewards businesses that offer quality, professionalism, and a genuine commitment to customer satisfaction.

With the knowledge and strategies outlined in this guide, you are now equipped to navigate the complexities of the UK market and position your business for long-term success. As you embark on your journey, remember that adaptability, consistency, and a focus on building lasting relationships are key to thriving in the UK.

Good luck with your business journey in the United Kingdom, and may your venture flourish as you unlock all that this vibrant and diverse market has to offer!

ABOUT THE AUTHOR

J K Lewis

J K Lewis has spent the past 30 years working, travelling and successfully selling in countries all around the world. He has lived in the UK, Germany and in South Korea; business has taken him all around Europe, the US and America, Asia and the MEA region. His sales and marketing experience covers a wide range of Products  and Services, from High-value German Engineering, to UK made special machinery, American Quality Management Services, to Chinese packaging and labels.

www.ingramcontent.com/pod-product-compliance
Lightning Source LLC
Chambersburg PA
CBHW052338220526
45472CB00001B/477